HORRIBLE SCIENCE

TEACHERS' RESOURCES

MINIBEASTS

Nick Arnold • Tony De Saulles
additional material David Tomlinson

AUTHOR
Nick Arnold

ILLUSTRATIONS
Tony De Saulles

ADDITIONAL MATERIAL
David Tomlinson

EDITOR
Wendy Tse

ASSISTANT EDITOR
Charlotte Ronalds

SERIES DESIGNER
Joy Monkhouse

DESIGNER
Erik Ivens

This book contains extracts from *Ugly Bugs, Suffering Scientists* and *The Awfully Big Quiz Book* in the Horrible Science series. Text © 1996, 2000, 2000, Nick Arnold. Illustrations © 1996, 2000, 2000, Tony De Saulles. First published by Scholastic Children's Books. Additional text © 2004, David Tomlinson.

Designed using Adobe InDesign

Published by Scholastic Ltd
Villiers House
Clarendon Avenue
Leamington Spa
Warwickshire
CV32 5PR

www.scholastic.co.uk

Printed by Bell & Bain Ltd, Glasgow

3 4 5 6 7 8 9   5 6 7 8 9 0 1 2 3 4

British Library Cataloguing-in-Publication Data
A catalogue record for this book is available from the British Library.

ISBN 0-439-97185-3
ISBN 978-0439-97185-0
The right of David Tomlinson to be identified as the Author of additional text of this Work has been asserted by him in accordance with the Copyright, Designs and Patents Act 1988.

TEACHERS' NOTES

Horrible Science Teachers' Resources: Minibeasts is inspired by the Horrible Science book *Ugly Bugs*. Each photocopiable page takes a weird and wonderful excerpt from the original, as well as material from *Suffering Scientists* and *The Awfully Big Quiz Book*, and expands on it to create a class-based teaching activity, fulfilling both National Curriculum and QCA objectives. The activities can be used individually or in a series as part of your scheme of work.

With an emphasis on research, experimentation and interpreting results, the activities will appeal to anyone even remotely curious about the Horrible world around us!

PART 1:
INTRODUCING MINIBEASTS

Pages 11 & 12: Ugly Bug Olympics & What's the score?
Learning objective
To record and interpret observations.
To use and present appropriate methods of research effectively.
To use available sources.

Start this session by asking your class what they know about any bugs that they may have come across outside or in the home. Allow any anecdotal tales of ant invasion and link this to any observations about how these creatures moved. Use photocopiable page 11 to explain that although bugs seem to us to be small and weak, they can do things relative to their size and that no human could do. Use photocopiable page 12 to stage your own Ugly Bug Olympics, linking the events to any maths work you may have done on measuring and division. For the weights testing use classroom objects, such as books or maths weights, that can be weighed or estimated first. This is not a test of the outer limits of the child's strength so no need for lead weights! Encourage your class to work with a partner or in teams, and include a ceremony where each entrant receives a medal.

Page 13: Dreadful discoveries
Learning objective
To ask scientific questions.

Start with a discussion about what the children already know about minibeasts and compile a list of minibeasts. Create a class list of questions to which the children would like to discover the answers.

Use photocopiable page 13 to introduce the idea that scientific research is a mixture of choice and chance. Scientists decide an area in which they are interested and plan how they will learn more, through observation and experiment. Chance can often help them learn more than they bargained for – like finding out that a worm that has been cut in half can become two worms! Explain that it is likely the children will learn about minibeasts through both choice and chance, and that the starting point for this is to plan some research. They can work individually or in pairs to choose a minibeast, draw it for a class gallery, and compile a list of questions to research. Ask them to use photocopiable page 13 to record their questions and refer to it as the topic progresses.

Page 14: Tough jobs
Learning objective
Enquiry in environmental and technological contexts.

Start this session by showing the children a Yellow Pages directory. Ask them to find a variety of services, explaining that humans take on different jobs to help each other as well as to earn a living. Use the adverts on photocopiable page 14 to introduce the concept that different creatures have different jobs, even though we may not be aware of them. Encourage your class to do research using books and the internet, as well as use their own knowledge, and to add their own entries to a class Yucky Yellow Pages directory of minibeast jobs and services.

Pages 15 & 16: A disgusting discovery & Drastic drama

Learning objective

To present information successfully.

Use photocopiable page 15 as the basis for a class reading session. Refer to the idea that scientists do not always know what they are about to observe or discover. Encourage the children to work in groups to form a prediction about what was found within the worm and compare their ideas.

Use the story as the basis for a class play; photocopiable page 16 will help the children write their scripts. Make the drama complete with audience participation. Encourage the children to take on non-human roles and to research what creatures might be found in the sea. Use music to convey the mood and perform the play for a neighbouring class or in a school assembly.

Answer: c) A slimy mass of billions of bacteria. The same disgusting chemical-guzzling bacteria that made the water cloudy. But here comes the surprise. The worms weren't actually eating the bacteria! Inside the worms' guts, the bacteria ate the smelly chemicals in the water and made new chemicals that the worms could feed off. Quite a cosy arrangement really.

Page 17: An Intellig-ant man

Learning objective

To ask scientific questions.

To make predictions of animals in their habitat.

Use the story of Baron Lubbock's experiment to look at how experiments are designed, focusing on the choices that scientists make. In this case the Baron chose to isolate the ants so that he could observe them without them wandering off or being threatened by other creatures. Encourage the children to decide what they would like to discover about ants and to plan an experiment. For example, they could try to find out what kind of foods they prefer or how they forage for food (do they lead other ants to it or do they hoard it for themselves?). Encourage the use of scientific words (such as equipment, method, prediction, results and conclusion).

Answers: 1, 2, 3 and **5** are true. **4** is false.

Page 18: Awesome ants!

Learning objective

To make predictions of animals in their habitat.

Start this session by recapping any work you may have done about ants and the jobs that they do. Use photocopiable page 18 to add more information, encouraging the children to add their own experiences. Talk about different smells and how they affect how we feel (for instance, walking past a chip shop often triggers hunger pangs even when we have not long had our dinner!). Link this to the activity and compare answers and ideas, for example how smell can be a form of communication for ants.

Answers: 1 d) 2 g) 3 f) 4 h) 5 b) 6 a).

Page 19: Beat the Baron!

Learning objective

To make predictions of animals in their habitat.

To treat animals with care and sensitivity.

To use available sources.

Talk to your class about what Baron Lubbock did when he was trying to discover more about ants. Focus on his use of observation, encouraging the children to pose their own questions about ants and their behaviour. Use an ant farm (these can be ordered, complete with ants, from most educational science companies) and set it up in your class. Talk to the children beforehand about respect for other creatures and agree a set of ant farm rules that everyone will abide by. Use the children's observations to form a class diary. They should observe the start of an ant building-spree within hours of the farm being set up. Encourage the children to take it in turns to report regularly from the ant farm on the latest developments.

Pages 20 & 21: Serious sorting: Bring on the beasts! & Unleashing the key!

Learning objective

To use available sources.

To use keys to identify animals.

Start this session by asking the children to sort some shapes on your table, either by colour or symmetry or number of sides. Ask them the criteria they chose and link this to any sorting work that you may have done previously. Cut up the cards on photocopiable page 20 and ask the children to get into groups and sort the cards, deciding their own criteria. Compare the criteria each group chose, highlighting any differences. Use photocopiable page 21 to introduce the concept of a sorting tree, encouraging the children to use the tree to sort the cards. The options on the tree are not exhaustive so encourage any children who wish to add additional questions or design a new tree of their own, especially to accommodate their own choice of minibeasts.

PART 2:

OBSERVING AND CLASSIFYING

Page 22: Savage spiders
Learning objective
To research using appropriate materials.

Start this session by talking to the children about their experiences with spiders. Some are likely to have a negative view. Use photocopiable page 22 to introduce the idea that spiders do a variety of jobs and come in all shapes and sizes. Use any pictures from books or the internet to introduce a variety of spiders to the children. The quiz on the photocopiable will introduce the children to some new and exciting attributes of spiders.
Answers: 1 b) 2 b) Tarantulas can live this long. **3** All of these! **4 c) 5 b) 6 c)** Sometimes it's a length of silk and sometimes a silken loop that acts just like a parachute. **7 b)** A spider's bite is supposed to make you dance madly – that's called tarantism. The tarantella folk dance is supposed to cure a bite. **8 b)** Scientists reckon there are two billion spiders in England and Wales! **9 b)** The spider drops in for a drink of water. But the walls of the bath are too slippery for the spider to climb out again.

Page 23: Weird webs
Learning objective
To present information successfully.
To record observations.
To apply scientific knowledge.

Start this session by talking to the children about patterns around us that are made just using straight lines (for example, tartan or check). Explain that webs are made using single threads in a pattern,

which the spider uses for a variety of reasons. Use photocopiable page 23 to introduce the concept that webs have different forms and functions. Start the activities with a pencil and ruler before graduating to thread, using nail boards as a base. Encourage the children to think of their own webs, focusing on the mathematical precision involved in a successful design.

Page 24: Being a butterfly
Learning objective
Presenting information successfully.
Recording observations.
Applying scientific knowledge.

Start this session by talking to your class about life processes, and how they started out as babies and developed as they grew older. Link this to other mammals and then to other creatures. Refer to any stories the children may be aware of (for example, *The Very Hungry Caterpillar* (Puffin)) and introduce the word 'metamorphosis', explaining that this means 'complete change' as opposed to the developing changes that humans and other mammals experience. Use photocopiable page 24 to focus the children on the life process of a butterfly and ask the children to design their own wings, recapping any work you may have done on shape and colour symmetry.
Answers: 1 a) Waste not – want not. **2 b) 3 a)** It's true! The caterpillar produces its own honey-like substance. **4 c) 5 b) 6 c)**.

Page 25: Irritating insects
Learning objective
To use words that name features of animals.
To use keys to identify animals.

Start this session by asking for a volunteer to stand at the front of the class. Ask the children to make labels for the major human body parts and to attach them to your volunteer. Talk to the children about how although different creatures may have different body parts, there can also be similarities. Compare the body parts of your volunteer to those of another mammal familiar to your class. Use photocopiable page 25 to introduce the idea that insect bodies are divided into different parts with different names. Use either pictures or safely sealed examples of insects (don't forget to give any live examples breathing holes and agree basic respect rules with the children beforehand). Encourage the children to share knowledge in a plenary session at the end.

Page 26: Down to earthworms
Learning objective
To treat animals with care and sensitivity.
To make predictions of animals in their habitat.

Worms, like spiders, can provoke a strong reaction in even the most mild-mannered human. Talk to the children about any experiences they may have had and any observations they have made. Use photocopiable page 26 as the starting point to look closely at earthworms and the jobs they do. If you have any live examples (again, carefully boxed with air holes and some soil) use them for this observation. Make sure that the children understand that they must not touch the worms under any circumstances. Like ant farms, worm farms are also available from educational science companies. Otherwise use any pictures from books and the internet for this activity, encouraging the children to describe what they observe in detail and to swap ideas. When deciding the length of the worms, invite your class to estimate and explain that this is a 'clever guess'.

Page 27: Are you an earthworm expert?
Learning objective
To treat animals with care and sensitivity.
To make predictions of animals in their habitat.

Recap any work you may have done previously observing earthworms, and use photocopiable page 27 to focus the children on the hidden life that we literally walk above each day. Encourage your class to work on their answers in groups, giving reasons for their conclusions. Share these ideas at the end and record good hypotheses, whether they were correct or not, in order to illustrate the value of creative thought in scientific research.
Answers: 1 c) Amazingly enough. **2 a)** *and* **b)**! Trick question, sorry. **3 b)** This makes the soil level rise and things level with the soil sink down. **4 c)** It was a type of giant earthworm that lives in South Africa. This monster wriggled out of the ground in Transvaal in 1937. **5 c)** The saddle is a belt that moves the length of the worm picking up the fertilised eggs. The worm wriggles free leaving the eggs in a cocoon.
6 b) 7 Another trick question. The answer is all three! **a)** Moles love a juicy earthworm. **b)** When they're full they bite their heads off and put them in their 'pantry'. This doesn't kill the worms it just stops them escaping! **c)** But sometimes a worm has time to grow another head and escape!

Page 28: Busy bees
Learning objective
To apply scientific knowledge.
To research using appropriate materials.

Bees are hard-working model citizens with a strict code of conduct! Talk to the children about patterns of behaviour in humans and what we call 'community'. Explain that, like us, bees work for the common good and survival. Encourage your class to recreate a bee community for five minutes. Divide the class into workers, drones and a queen; give each child a sticky label showing their status. Mark out an area of the classroom to represent the hive. Use photocopiable page 28 to focus them on the different jobs carried out by the bees in their hive community. Encourage your class to work in a confined space but without pushing each other around. Explain that although bees do crawl over each other it is in an orderly way! At the end of the five minutes ask the children how they felt about working in a hive community. You can extend this activity to become a drama piece and to make a model of a hive for a class display. Ensure that the children understand that hives are man made and that in the wild bees live in nests in much the same way.

Page 29: Horrible honey
Learning objective
To use available sources.
Scientific investigation.

Start this session by showing the children a jar of honey with the honeycomb in it (this is available from most supermarkets). Explain that honeycomb is made of wax secreted by worker bees as they go about their jobs. The weight and pressure of the honeycomb forms the wax into six-sided shapes (don't give the mathematical term away at this point) which hold the runny honey in place in the hive. Split the children into groups and ask them to look, touch and describe the honey and its comb, explaining that although it is a food (and honeycomb is a natural antibiotic) we never ever eat anything being used in scientific experimentation. Use photocopiable page 29 to record the children's observations and encourage mathematical terms such as 'tessellation' and 'equal' when looking at the comb.

Page 30: Terrible table manners!
Learning objective
To use and present appropriate methods of research effectively.
To use simple apparatus to observe.
Scientific investigation.

Start this session by eating an apple in front of your class, asking them to describe the method that humans use to eat. Compare this with other animals that they know about. Use photocopiable page 30 to focus the children on the concept that even very small insects eat and drink and that there are similarities as well as differences in the way they do this when compared to humans. Encourage your class to carry out the experiment, recording their observations as they do so and comparing notes at the end.

PART 3:

INVESTIGATING AND APPLYING

Pages 31 & Page 32: Disgusting designs 1 & 2
Learning objective
To use words that name features of animals.
To use keys to identify animals.
Role of habitat and reproduction in development.

Start this session by looking at pictures or live examples of beetles. Recap any work you may have done about identifying animal or human body parts. Use photocopiable page 31 to look in detail at how insects are constructed. Encourage your class to talk about the differences and similarities they notice between insects and other animals, including humans. Talk about scale as well as the body parts themselves. Use photocopiable page 32 to help the children design their own insects. The objective here is for the children to understand the main body parts and to appreciate the role that habitat and reproduction have to all living things. Explain that a habitat is a place where a living thing can find food, shelter and everything else it needs for daily life. Encourage your class to be imaginative and to draw pictures as detailed as photocopiable page 31. Have a class insectarium, with each child presenting their creature, complete with information. Extend this activity by making models of the insects for a class display.

Page 33: Nasty nursery rhymes
Learning objective
Scientific investigation.

Begin by asking your class about the nursery rhymes they remember from when they were younger. Introduce the 'Ladybird, ladybird' rhyme on photocopiable page 33. Originally this rhyme was a satirical verse aimed at mothers who drank too much gin and abandoned their children! However, for the purposes of this lesson, explain that the rhyme is incorrect in its observations of ladybirds and their behaviour. Challenge the children to improve on the rhyme using knowledge they have acquired. Compare examples and broaden the challenge so that other rhymes about insects can be updated more scientifically. Use these rhymes for a class book and invite some younger children to give their verdict.

Page 34: Manic metamorphosis: The movie
Learning objective
Scientific investigation.
Adults have young and that these grow into adults, which in turn produce young.

Recap any work that your class may have done about the changes that occur when a caterpillar becomes a butterfly. Use the word 'metamorphosis' and define it as 'complete change'. Use photocopiable page 34 to focus your class on the distinct stages of this process. Explain that they will get the opportunity to make their own movie using flick books. You will need booklets of about 8 square cm with a minimum of 30 sheets in each, stapled securely. Explain that the booklets need so many pictures because the rate at which the book is flicked means each image is seen for only a fraction of a second. The children can either work individually or in groups where each team member produces a book for one part of the process and then the whole team put their books together to make a blockbuster! Encourage the children to design covers for the books and posters that will make audiences want to see the contents.

Pages 35 & 36: Ugly bug parade 1 & 2
Learning objective
To present information successfully.
To record observations.
To apply scientific knowledge.

Use photocopiable pages 35 and 36 to discuss the wide variety of insects around us. Cut up the insect cards and ask the children to work in pairs to find out as much as they can about that example. Explain that an Ugly Bug Parade will take place in school and that each pair will represent a different bug. Use chicken wire or modelling twigs along with papier mâché to make the finished models. Alternatively, incorporate the models into funky headgear or full costume. Encourage the children to be as accurate as possible and to also create scale models of flowers, hives, webs and so on, and to choose appropriate music. Stage your Ugly Bug Parade as part of a school fair, open day or assembly. Ask the children to take on the role of the insect they represent and to be able to answer basic questions that audience members may have for them. Use photographs from the parade as part of a class display alongside the costumes and research notes.

Pages 37 & 38: Ugly Bug Debate & The campaign trail!
Learning objective
To present information successfully.
To record observations.
To apply scientific knowledge.

Organise a class debate around the motion 'Should bugs be banned?' Write a brief news report along the lines of: 'Following protests from people who have been stung by bees, scared by spiders and sickened by slugs in their salad, a new law is planned to ban all bugs'. Ask a responsible volunteer to act as newsreader to read the 'breaking news' to the rest of the class. Explain that the children will now have the chance to debate the new law, and outline the basic rules for the debate. The newsreader will be the chairperson, and two debate teams are needed to propose and oppose the motion. Encourage your class to use information from recent work to support their points of view (for example: Against – some insects do vital jobs; For – flies can spread disease). Use photocopiable page 37 to focus possible points for debate, encouraging your class to include their own research. Each debate team should plan and write a persuasive speech to be read out by the spokesperson. Photocopiable page 38 has other excellent information that may be useful, as well as ideas for campaign material. The rest of the class

should take on different roles (such as a scientist, animal rights activist, farmers, and so on). They should think about both sides of the arguments and write down questions that they can ask either team. At the end of the debate, once everyone has spoken, take a class vote using an anonymous paper ballot and ask the chairperson to announce the results.

Page 39: Mysterious malaria
Learning objective
To make predictions and generalisations relating to patterns in data.
Interdependence and survival.

Begin this session by talking about travelling overseas and that sometimes we need vaccinations to protect us from diseases in other countries. Introduce the link between mosquitoes and the spread of malaria. Explain that there are different strains of malaria and that today we have treatments to relieve the symptoms but it used to be a great killer. Malarial deaths are relatively rare today where adequate medical supplies are close at hand and treatment administered swiftly. In times of natural disaster or in extremely poor countries, rates of malaria are much higher. Talk to the children about the period in which the cartoon on photocopiable page 39 is set. The British Empire was at its peak and people from Britain worked overseas in large numbers for the first time. Malaria was greatly feared but people did not know how it was transmitted. Mosquitoes breed in stagnant (non-running) water; this can include a cup of fresh water, a puddle of rain, or a pond. They feed on blood and some types can transmit diseases such as malaria or infections when they bite. Recap any work that you may have done in English regarding adapting stories into plays and use the tips on photocopiable page 39 to encourage your class to write a play telling the story of the mystery of malaria. Use the play as an opportunity to perform in assembly for other classes.

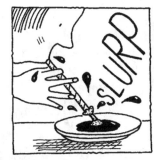

Page 40: Bug safety
Learning objective
To record and interpret observations.
To use and present appropriate methods of research effectively.

Start by asking the children for anecdotal tales of things they did when they were younger. Encourage any tales involving eating something that should not have been eaten, stressing how dangerous it is. Talk to the children about some of the safety lessons they have learned regarding foods and plants and insects. Use photocopiable page 40 to introduce the idea that the children in your class are now in charge of a safety campaign aimed at younger children. List the ideas that they have and discuss how this may be presented so that it is accessible. Talk about respecting minibeasts' habitat as an important part of staying safe (such as not stamping on an ants nest or disturbing a bees nest). Other safety points could include information about how we react to nuisance minibeasts (such as staying calm and still if a wasp is around instead of aggravating it by swatting). Use the posters as the basis for slogans, songs, poems or banners and produce a presentation for younger children from another class.

Page 41: Maria Merien's world of brilliant bugs
Learning objective
That there are different types of animals in the immediate environment.
To ask scientific questions.

Talk to your class about the bravery involved in taking a long trip in Maria Merien's lifetime; in those days medical knowledge was limited and many people died of tropical diseases that can be cured or prevented today. Look at Maria Merien's letter to her former husband. Encourage the children to look up the area she visited and the distance from her home in the Netherlands. Ask your class to draft a reply to Maria telling her all about the bugs, climate and habitats that we see in this country so that she can contrast it to where she is. Use the 'Bet you never knew!' section as an opportunity to look closely at similar insects that could go together and form 'Horrible Hybrids'.

Page 42: Lethal lepidopterists
Learning objective
To recognise ways in which living things need protection.
To use and present appropriate methods of research effectively.

Use photocopiable page 42 to introduce the concept of responsible investigation. People no longer 'collect' butterflies by killing them, just as photographic safaris have largely seen the extinction of safaris where people slaughtered wildlife and turned them into rugs and hat stands. Recap any work your class may have done about butterflies and encourage them to add their own questions.
Answers: 1 c) All the others are generally true but not always. **2 a)** One head is just a decoy. A horrible hunter thinks it's bitten off the butterfly's head. Instead all it's got is a mouthful of wing. **3 c)** The hot liquid loosened the strands of silk. **4 b) 5 a)** Old butterflies have actually been around for just a few weeks. They hardly ever live much longer.

PART 4:
ASSESSMENT AND QUIZ

Pages 43 & 44: Plague Puzzle 1 & 2
Learning objective
To make predictions and generalisations relating to patterns in data.

Use photocopiable page 43 to introduce the story of the Great Plague. Ask for volunteers to sing 'Ring-a-roses' explaining that it is about the deaths from plague that decimated populations at this time. Use the options at the end of the story to introduce the term 'hypothesis'; when scientists are searching for the truth there is no right or wrong answer, just hypotheses. Explain to the children that a hypothesis is an unproved idea to explain why something happens. Great discoveries have come from hypotheses but each one has to be tested by experiment or observation. Ask the children to work in groups or pairs, using photocopiable page 44 to record their hypotheses in cartoon strip form. Bring the groups together at the end of the session to swap ideas and reveal the answer.
Answer: b) Microbes multiply in the flea's gut until it can't feed. The hungry flea bites a human and injects millions of germs.

Although Simond had the answer it took another 20 years before scientists accepted that he was right. It wasn't until 1914 that they fully understood the effects of the plague on fleas. Already vaccines were being developed against the plague and these together with insecticides and rat poisons have reduced the danger of plague epidemics in the future.

Page 45: Incredible bug discoveries quiz
Learning objective

To apply scientific knowledge.
To research using appropriate materials.

Use photocopiable page 45 to start a class quiz. Split your children into mixed-ability teams, each taking on the name of a favourite insect. The emphasis in this activity is on the children researching quiz questions to add to the ones on the sheet. Encourage the children to come up with a mix of two- and three-point questions and play in the style of a television game show.
Answers:
The made-up places are...
c) There are no active volcanoes in Switzerland.
e) The heat of the light would kill any bugs or microbes.
The others are true...
a) Scientists have found strange new types of microbes living in the ice just above the lake and nicknamed them 'Mickey Mouse' and 'Klingon'. The scientists believe that the water may be home to microbes that have been lost to the world for 25 million years.
b) The symbion (sim-be-on), first spotted in 1995, is just 1 mm long. In fact, people who eat lobsters have been scoffing the bugs for years without noticing!
d) The xeno (ze-no) is a tiny insect with 100 eyes. Despite all the studies of wasps over the years, no one noticed the xeno until 1995, but I guess the xeno's had its eyes on us.

Page 46: Unbelievable beetles!
Learning objective

To treat animals with care and sensitivity.
To apply scientific knowledge.

If you have access to live beetles of any common species (carefully protected in breathable boxes) then you can use them to introduce the activity on

photocopiable page 46. You can use this as the second round of the quiz in the activity on photocopiable page 45 or as a separate activity of its own. Ensure that the children have access to books and the Internet to set their own questions and encourage them to set others based on their own observations of the beetles in class.
Answers: 1 True. **2** True. But they are more usually found on tobacco plants. **3** True. **4** False. Even beetles can't survive extreme cold. **5** True. **6** True. It is especially fond of traditional medicines made from dried plants. **7** False. Beetles don't use mouthwash. **8** True. But you could always fry the beetle instead of the bacon. **9** True. The visitors have to view living beetles instead. **10** True.

Page 47: Insect news quiz
Learning objective

To apply scientific knowledge.
To research using appropriate materials.

Use the activity on photocopiable page 47 as the next round of a mega-class quiz or as an activity in its own right. Encourage the children to set their own spot-the-mistake questions. As an extension, they could write and design their own insect newspaper.
Answers: 1 Ants, like all other insects, have six feet, not five. **2** Slugs don't make poison gas. **3** Spider webs are made from spider's silk not fly guts. The spider makes its silk out of old webs that it's eaten. It can re-use the chemicals that make the web in just 30 minutes. **4** You won't see the Southern Lights in the Arctic, but you might see the Northern Lights.

Page 48: Ugly bug quiz
Learning objective

To make predictions.
To make generalisations relating to patterns in data.

Use the activity on photocopiable page 48 to encourage the children to work on their own or in pairs, giving reasons for their answers. Although the quiz simply asks 'true or false?' this is an excellent opportunity for the children to ask 'why?' and to think of some possible reasons. Encourage hypotheses by suggesting wild ideas of your own so that the children can feel secure if hypotheses of their own are not factually correct. The emphasis here is on encouraging confidence and valuing contribution.

NAME _____   DATE _____

Ugly Bug Olympics

Since the day that a caveman or cavewoman first squashed a cockroach there has been a non-stop war between ugly bugs and humans. It's the biggest war the world has ever known.

You might think that humans have an advantage over insects. A human is far bigger than the biggest insect. So humans can easily squash the insect. Humans are more intelligent than insects. (Well, *most* humans are!) But if you look at what humans and insects can do for their size the picture is very different.

Ugly Bug Olympics

Running *Winner:* One species of cockroach can run 50 times its body length in one second. *Loser:* The fastest human to run 50 times his own body length (about 80 metres) was about ten times slower.

The high jump *Winner:* Fleas can jump 30 cm – that's 130 times their own height. *Loser:* To match that a human would have to jump 250 metres into the air!

The long jump *Winner:* Jumping spiders can leap 40 times their body length. *Runner-up:* Grasshoppers can leap 20 times their own body length. *Loser:* To match that a human would have to leap the length of nine London buses in a single jump!

Weight-lifting *Winner:* Scarab beetles can lift weights 850 times heavier than their own bodies. *Loser:* To equal that a human would have to lift eight London buses at the same time!

Walking on the ceiling *Winner:* Flies. *Loser:* Humans can't do this at all.

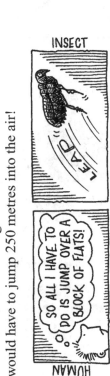

Bet you never knew!
Termites build gigantic nests. One nest contained 11,750 tonnes of sand. The termites had piled it up grain by grain and stuck it all together with spit! Beat that – humans!

NAME _____   DATE _____

What's the score?

Event 1: Running

Run as **far** as you can in 60 seconds. Measure the distance with a trundle wheel. Divide the distance by 60 to calculate how far you ran in one second.

My total distance: _____

My distance per second: _____

Event 2: High jump

Jump as **high** as you can from a crouching position. Ask your partner to measure the height with a metre stick. Try it three times and take the average.

My three high jumps: _____

My average: _____

Event 3: Long jump

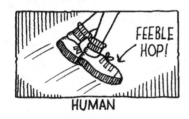

Jump as **far** as you can after a run up. Ask your partner to measure the distance with a tape measure. Try it three times and take the average.

My three long jumps: _____

My average: _____

Event 4: Weight lifting

Choose two objects from the weights table. Lift one and then put it down. Now lift the other. Add these two weights together for your total.

Weight one: _____

Weight two: _____

Total: _____

Event 5: Walking on the ceiling

DON'T EVEN TRY IT!

Congratulations on completing the Ugly Bug Olympics – now design a Gold medal for your achievements!

NAME _____   DATE _____

Dreadful discoveries

Imagine any plant or animal or microbe. If it's alive we want to know how it lives and if it's dead we may want to cut it up and find out what's inside it.

Plant scientists = botanists
Animal scientists = zoologists
Scientists who study how plants and animals live together in an area = ecologists

Me, I'm a flatworm person. I love them and all their fascinating little ways. Did you know you can cut one in half and it becomes two worms? I'm at university studying how a new brain forms in the back end of the worm — fascinating! My idea of a fun day out is to get stuck into a nice, smelly mud flat and study the worms in their natural home.

● Take a look at the minibeasts in your class gallery.

● What would you like to discover about them?

● Write your questions here as you think of them.

_____

_____

_____

_____

_____

● Now that you know what you want to find out, think about where you might find it and how you will present your findings.

● You could write a booklet, draw a strip cartoon, compose a song or poem, compile your own 'Bet you never knew' fact file – or any other way you can think of!

NAME _____ DATE _____

TOUGH JOBS

Sexton Beetle *and Sons and Daughters*

Dead? Just call in your friendly family funeral directors. No job too large. We'll bury anything even if it means ten hour shifts. Free personal limb chopping service to make burials easier. Professional after-care service. Our little grubs will look after the grave. No fee charged but they do like to come to the funeral feast. That's to feast on the dead body of course!

- Those beetles have been working very hard.
- Here are some more minibeasts. Draw them and find out what sort of jobs they do. Do the same for a minibeast of your choice.

Black Widow spider

Jobs:

Bee

Jobs:

Ant

Jobs:

My minibeast

Jobs:

Got a tough job? Get a beetle to do it
Beetles don't only come in a horrible variety of shapes and sizes. They also have a mind-boggling array of lifestyles, and where there's a job to be done there's a beetle at the ready.

ELM BARK BEETLE TREE SURGEON
Unsightly elm trees getting you down? Need a bit more light? Call us now. Try our unique Dutch elm disease fungus formula – a revolting little rootless plant that terminates trees. We'll soon get in under the bark and wipe out the woody weeds!
▲ Forest felled.
▲ No job too large.
Disease established in UK – 1970s. Over 25 million elms eliminated.

BEWARE! IT'S A BOMBARDIER!
Get yourself the ultimate in personal self-defence systems! Beat off the bullies with a bombardier beetle gun. Unique self-mixing action for nasty boiling chemicals. Amazing internal heating system in abdomen heats chemicals to temperature of 100°C and fires at 500 to 1000 squirts a second! The bombardier beetle gun is maintenance free. Just let it crunch on a few smaller insects now and then.

BRIGHTEN UP YOUR HOME
With a firefly lantern. As used in Brazil, the West Indies and Far East. Firefly lanterns cast a soft green or yellow light from the bodies of female fireflies. Forty fireflies are as bright as one candle. They need no power or batteries – it's all done with chemicals by your friendly firefly.

- Write and design adverts for their services to make a Yucky Yellow Pages directory of minibeast services.

NAME _____ DATE _____

A disgusting discovery

The Pacific Ocean off the Galapagos Islands, 1977

There was definitely something down there. Something strange and terrifying. Instruments trailing from the research ship far into the depths below revealed strange rises in sea temperature. Cameras lowered into the deep-sea darkness had taken pictures of strange shapes. And water samples taken from the deep stank enough to make you sick. The scientists needed to know more. Someone had to visit those remote depths where no human had ever been before. But what would they find when they got there?

Metre by metre the submersible slipped ever deeper into the unknown. From the observation window the scientists could make out nothing but the pitch-black freezing cold sea. The surface of the Pacific Ocean was a terrifying 2.5 km above their heads. And on every square centimetre of the submersible, a tonne of ocean pressed down. In the lights of the tiny craft the scientists could see strange volcanic rocks. But no sign of life. They shivered. Nothing could live down here in this horrible place surely? Then it happened.

The submersible's temperature gauge spun off the scale with a gigantic heat surge. The water turned from black to cloudy blue. The scientists had found a natural chimney that led deep beneath the earth's surface. Here, heated chemicals, stinking like rotten eggs, boil up from below at terrifically high temperatures. And the hot cloudy water was alive with bacteria too small for the eye to see. The billions of bacteria billowed in vast clouds. Strange ghostly pale crabs scurried through the ooze on the sea bed in search of bits of drowned sea creatures. And

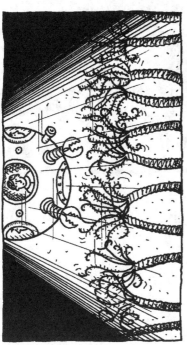

there were thousands of giant clams. Then out of the darkness and confusion, the THINGS appeared.

The scientists were astounded. What were these creatures? Were they alien life-forms? Why did they look so weird? The strange red tips of the creatures waved in the sea. Their bodies were hidden in long white upright tubes, each 4 metres long, and they had red blood just like humans. They were giant seaworms – the largest ever seen and of a type unknown to science. But these ugly bugs had no mouths and no stomachs. So how and what did they eat?

There was only one way to find out. The robot arm of the submersible reached out and grabbed a worm from its strange home. Back on the ship a fearless scientist sliced it open. What do you think he found inside?

a) crabs

b) bits of dead animal that had floated down from the surface.

c) beastly bacteria

● Discuss what you think was found inside the worm with your group. Write your ideas here:

NAME _____   DATE _____

Drastic drama

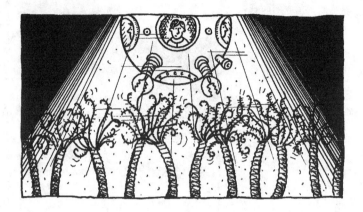

- Take a look at the story of 'A disgusting discovery'.

- Use the story as the basis for your play. Your adaptation should include **characters** (don't forget to give them names!), **dialogue, stage directions** and action split into **scenes**. Don't forget that your **cast** can play the **roles** of sea life as well as humans.

- Try and include a lot of movement to set the scene, and choose music that will help you build up a spooky atmosphere.

- To make the drama interactive, stop the action when it gets to the part about cutting open the worm and ask your audience what they think was found inside. You could give them some choices and take an audience vote!

My characters:

Music:

Costumes and props:

Scene 1: location

Character name: Dialogue (include any stage directions in brackets)

NAME _____ DATE _____

An intellig-ant man

Almost as awesome as the ants themselves, are some of the humans who studied them. Take Baron Lubbock, for example. . .

Baron Lubbock (1834-1913) was an expert on everything. He wrote more than 25 books, and over 100 scientific reports.

He even gave lectures on . . .

Trade, the Alps, how crabs hear

He published books about . . .

FLOWERS — ROCKS
THE SCENERY ~OF~ SWITZERLAND

And those were just his hobbies. In politics he introduced . . .

. . .Bank holidays to Britain.

Hurrah!

He was an artist, too. Lubbock drew pictures for one of Charles Darwin's books on . . .

Barnacles

He travelled around Europe and studied . . .

Ancient rubbish tips

ROMAN BAKED BEANS

But all this was nothing compared to his life-long love affair – with insects.
The barmy baron devised an awesome ant experiment. . .

PULLEY FOR LOWERING THE ANTS NEST

AN ANTS NEST SANDWICHED BETWEEN TWO SHEETS OF GLASS

ANTS NEST IS LOWERED ONTO THE ISLAND

MOAT TO STOP ANTS ESCAPING FROM THE ISLAND

- What could Baron Lubbock discover from his experiment?

- Take a look at the picture above and think about why he designed the experiment this way. Consider why he isolated the ants on an island.

- Answer the quiz questions below and design an experiment of your own to discover more about ants.

- Here are some of his discoveries. They have been mixed up with some false statements. See if you can sort the true from the false.

1 Ants can be ancient. Worker ants can live for seven years and queen ants for 14.
2 Ants listen through their legs!
3 Ants can judge directions by using the sun's rays – even on a cloudy day!
4 Ants talk through their bums.
5 Ants are like sheep – they follow a leader ant in front who makes a trail.

NAME _____ DATE _____

AWESOME ANTS!

- Ants are amazing! Take a look at this fact file.

- Where have you seen ants? Write about your ant experiences below.

_____
_____
_____
_____
_____
_____

Name of creature:	Ant
Where found:	Worldwide on land. They always live in nests.
Distinguishing features:	Most ants are less than 1 cm long. Narrow waist between thorax and abdomen. Angled feelers.

FEELERS   WAIST   ← RIDICULOUSLY FAT ABDOMEN

ANT

Ant Aromas

Scents are very important to ants. Scientists have discovered several ant scents each of which makes ants do different things. Imagine you were a scientist observing different kinds of ant behaviour. Draw a line between the ants' behaviour and the aroma that causes it.

1 ALARM SMELL 2 NEST SMELL 3 TRAIL SMELL 4 QUEEN BREEDING TIME SMELL 5 BIG NASTY ENEMY SMELL 6 DEAD ANT SMELL

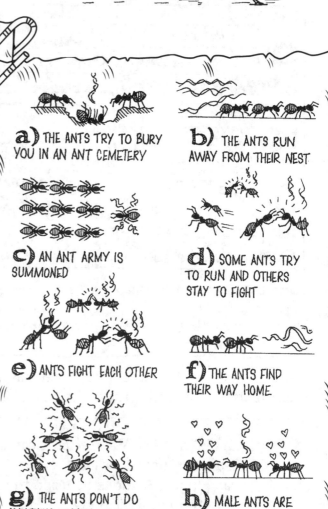

a) THE ANTS TRY TO BURY YOU IN AN ANT CEMETERY

b) THE ANTS RUN AWAY FROM THEIR NEST

c) AN ANT ARMY IS SUMMONED

d) SOME ANTS TRY TO RUN AND OTHERS STAY TO FIGHT

e) ANTS FIGHT EACH OTHER

f) THE ANTS FIND THEIR WAY HOME

g) THE ANTS DON'T DO ANYTHING IF YOU HAVE THIS SMELL

h) MALE ANTS ARE ATTRACTED BY THIS SMELL

Bet you never knew

There are 10,000 species of ant. But they do have some things in common.
- *An ant nest is ruled by a queen who spends her life laying eggs.*
- *All the ordinary 'worker' ants are female.*
- *Males only hatch out at mating time and they die once they have mated!*

NAME _____   DATE _____

Beat the Baron!

- Baron Lubbock loved ants! He designed this experiment to observe ants' behaviour.

- What can you discover? Look closely at your ants' nest. Draw and write your observations to find out about:

  1. Changes to the nest itself
  2. The ants' patterns of behaviour
  3. Differences in their behaviour at different times of day

Start of Day 1	End of Day 1	Day 2
Day 3	Day 7	Day 10

- Write your own intellig-ant diary to show Baron Lubbock a thing or two about ants that even he might have missed!

NAME _____ DATE _____

Serious sorting: Bring on the beasts!

● Cut out these minibeasts and add your own gruesome choices!

Caterpillar 	Butterfly 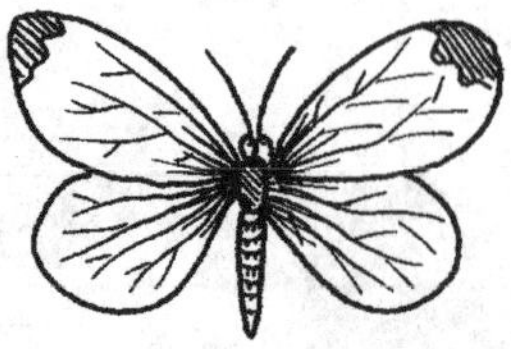	Dragonfly 	My choice:
CHOMP CHOMP			
My choice:	**Spider** 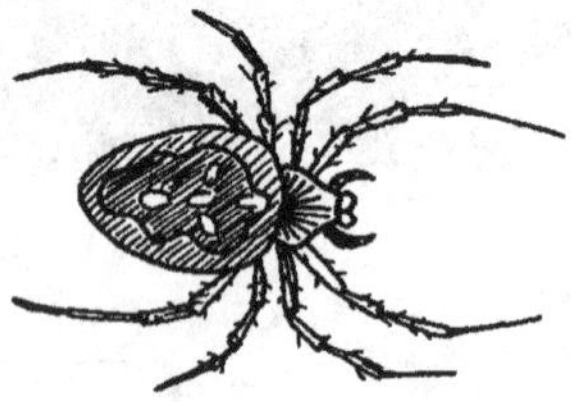	**Whirligig beetle** 	**Snail** 
Slug 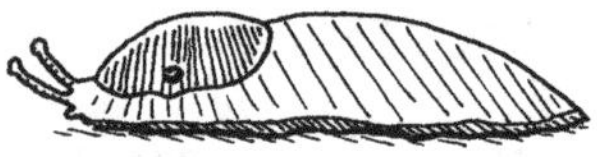	**My choice:**	**My choice:**	**My choice:**
My choice:	**Fly** 	**My choice:**	**Ant** 

● How do these minibeasts differ? How could you sort them? Think of some questions that you could ask that would help classify the minibeasts.

_____

_____

_____

_____

NAME _____   DATE _____

Serious sorting: Unleashing the key!

Does it have legs?

Yes! → How many legs does it have?

No! → Does it have a shell?

- **Yes!** It's a snail.
- **No!** It could be a slug, worm or larvae.

Six legs! Does it also have wings?

- **No!** It could be an ant or a certain type of aphid.
- **Yes! Two pairs that I can see really easily!** It could be a butterfly, moth, bee, wasp, mayfly, dragonfly or lacewing.
- **Yes! Two pairs, but one is hidden!** It could be a beetle or earwig.
- **Yes! One pair!** It could be a midge, mosquito or crane fly.

Eight legs! It's a spider.

More than eight legs! It could be a centipede, millipede or woodlouse.

Ugly bug families

The worst thing about ugly bugs is that there are so many of them. There are thousands and thousands of different types. They have to be sorted out before we can even begin to get to know them. It's a horrible job – but someone has to do it. Don't worry, though, it won't be you – here's a list some scientists prepared earlier.

Each type of living thing is called a species and these species are put into larger groups called genera, a bit like belonging to a club. Groups of genera make families. Confused yet? You will be.

A SPECIES →

A GROUP OF SPECIES MAKES A GENERA →

THIS GROUP OF GENERA MAKES A FAMILY →

- Use this key to help sort the creatures from 'Bring on the beasts!' You can add questions of your own to improve it.

NAME _____   DATE _____

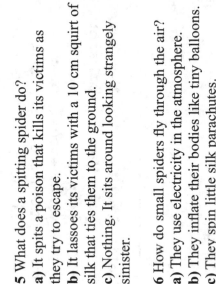
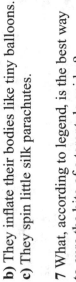
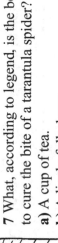
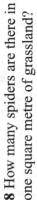

SAVAGE SPIDERS

Name of creature:	Spider
Where found:	Worldwide. On land and in fresh water.
Horrible habits:	Paralyses prey with poison fangs and sucks out the juices.
Any helpful habits:	Keeps down the numbers of insects.
Distinguishing features:	Head and thorax joined. Separate abdomen. Four pairs of jointed legs. Eight eyes. Produces silk. Inside is a breathing organ called a lung book.

Spider test of terror

1 How do spiders avoid getting caught in their own webs?
a) Nifty footwork.
b) They have oily non-stick feet.
c) They slide down a line and pulley.

2 How long can a spider live?
a) Six months.
b) 25 years.
c) 75 years.

3 When a spider sheds its skin what parts does it get rid of?
a) Its skin.
b) The front of its eyes.
c) The lining of its guts and lung book (breathing organ).

4 What does a spider do with its old web?
a) Wear it.
b) Throw it away.
c) Eat it.

5 What does a spitting spider do?
a) It spits a poison that kills its victims as they try to escape.
b) It lassoes its victims with a 10 cm squirt of silk that ties them to the ground.
c) Nothing. It sits around looking strangely sinister.

6 How do small spiders fly through the air?
a) They use electricity in the atmosphere.
b) They inflate their bodies like tiny balloons.
c) They spin little silk parachutes.

7 What, according to legend, is the best way to cure the bite of a tarantula spider?
a) A cup of tea.
b) A lively folk dance.
c) Suck out the venom.

8 How many spiders are there in one square metre of grassland?
a) 27.
b) 500.
c) 1,795.

9 How does a spider get into your bath?
a) It crawls up the drain-pipe but can't climb out of the bath.
b) It drops down from the ceiling but can't climb out of the bath.
c) It crawls out of the taps but can't climb out of the bath.

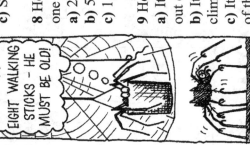
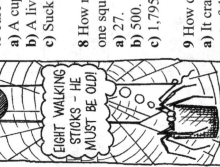

EIGHT WALKING STICKS – HE MUST BE OLD!

NAME _____   DATE _____

Weird webs

Spiders spin silk to produce their intricate webs. The webs they make catch flies and other unlucky creatures. But the more you find out about webs the weirder they seem.

1 To make one web, spiders need to spin different types of silk.

• Dry silk a thousandth of a millimetre thick for the spokes of a web.

• Stretchy silk covered in gluey droplets for the rest. The sticky bits take in moisture and stop the web drying out.

• Other kinds of silk for wrapping up eggs and dead insects.

2 Webs come in many shapes and sizes. Have you ever seen any of these?

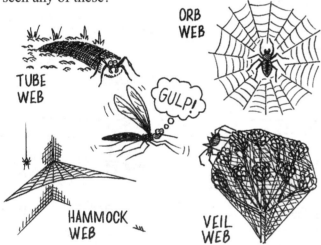

TUBE WEB

ORB WEB

GULP!

HAMMOCK WEB

VEIL WEB

3 The house spider makes a hammock-shaped web. The spider spits out bits of insect and leaves them lying around for someone else to tidy up – a horrible habit!

4 The trap-door spider digs a tunnel with a trap door at one end. The spider waits within. It grabs a passing insect and pulls it down. The door closes and the innocent victim is never seen again.

SHUT THE DOOR LOVE – THERE'S A TERRIBLE DRAUGHT COMING DOWN THE TUNNEL!

• Try making a similar web to the house spider.

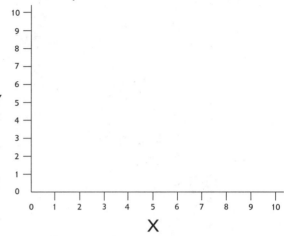

• Use a pencil and ruler to join y1 to x10, y2 to x9, y3 to x8, y4 to x7, y5 to x6, y6 to x5, y7 to x4, y8 to x3, y9 to x2 and y10 to x1.

• What do you notice?

_____

_____

• Look at the instructions again. What number pattern do you notice?

_____

_____

• If the axes both went up to 20cm, what would the next numbers be to continue this pattern? Continue the instructions and draw your new web.

• Look at your orb web. Work out how you could make it using cotton and tacks. Number each point and write instructions to help.

• Design your own web, explaining how it works and how it is made.

NAME _____   DATE _____

Being a butterfly

Could you be a large blue butterfly?
The large blue butterfly is – amazingly enough, a large, blue butterfly. In Britain it is very rare and is currently only found in a few places in the West Country. Large blue butterflies are also found in France and Central Europe.

Like all butterflies, the large blue begins life as an egg that hatches into a caterpillar that turns into a chrysalis that turns into a butterfly. But it does horribly odd things on the way. Imagine you were a large blue butterfly. Would you survive?

1 You hatch out. How do you get rid of the remains of your egg?
a) Eat it.
b) Bury it.
c) Throw it at a passing wasp.

2 You live on a wild thyme or marjoram plant. Suddenly your plant is invaded by another large blue caterpillar that starts eating your leaves. What do you do?
a) Agree to share the plant.
b) Eat the rival caterpillar.
c) Hide until it's gone away.

3 After guzzling all the leaves you can, and shedding your skin three times, you fall off your plant. As you amble along, an ant suddenly appears. What do you do?
a) Persuade it to give you a cuddle – then give it some honey in return.
b) Grip its feelers and refuse to let go.
c) Roll over and pretend to be dead.

4 The ant takes you to its nest. It shoves you in a chamber with the ant grubs. What do you do next?
a) Make friends with them.
b) Raid the ants' food supplies and help yourself.
c) Eat the ant grubs.

5 You spend the winter sleeping in the ants' nest. Soon after you wake you hang yourself from the ceiling and turn into a chrysalis.

About three weeks later you fall on the floor and crawl out of your nasty damp chrysalis. Congratulations – you're now an adult butterfly! But how do you escape from the ants' nest?
a) You have to dig an escape tunnel.
b) You crawl your way out all by yourself.
c) You pretend to be dead and an ant carries you out.

6 Free at last! What's the first thing you do?
a) Find something to eat – a dead ant will do.
b) Find a mate.
c) Dry out your brand new wet wings.

And then you fly off to enjoy your new life! Make the best of it – you've only got 15 days to live!

MUM, WHY IS THIS ANT LICKING ME?

IT'S A LONG STORY!

• Now design your wings here.

My butterfly wings

NAME _____   DATE _____

IRRITATING INSECTS

Insect bodies are divided into three parts – a head, a middle bit or thorax and a bit at the back called an abdomen. An insect has two feelers (antennae) on its head and three pairs of legs attached to its thorax. Scientists have identified about a million insect species with bodies like these and there are plenty more just waiting to be discovered.

- Take a look at your insects. Draw them as accurately as you can.

- Label the antennae, thorax and abdomen.

My observational drawings

NAME _____   DATE _____

DOWN TO EARTHWORMS

- Take a good look at your earthworms.

- Describe their colour, length and the way that they move.

Name of creature:	Earthworm
Where found:	Most soils worldwide
Distinguishing features:	Segmented body. See-through skin. Slides along by squeezing its body segments forward.

Are earthworms awful?
'Yes', according to people who don't like slimy wriggling creatures.
'No', according to some very famous naturalists.
Gilbert White wrote in 1770 . . .

Earthworms though in appearance a small and despicable link in the Chain of Nature, yet if lost would make a lamentable chasm.

Charles Darwin called earthworms . . .

Earthworms have played a most important part in the history of the world.

TAIL END   SADDLE →

I DIDN'T KNOW THAT!

HOW WORMS MOVE

HEAD END

- What's your opinion of earthworms?

_____
_____
_____
_____

My earthworm description

_____
_____
_____
_____

My earthworm drawing

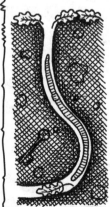

NAME _____   DATE _____

Are you an earthworm expert?

You may think that earthworms are deadly dull and boring. And of course, you'd be right. But delve a little deeper into their humdrum lives and you'll discover some slimy surprises. See if you can guess these answers.

1 How many worms could you count per hectare (2½ acres) of farmland?
a) Three.
b) 65,697.
c) Two million.

2 Why on earth do earthworms have bristles? (This is true. Just try stroking one – if you dare!)
a) To help them move along.
b) To stop the early bird from yanking them out of the soil.
c) To sweep their burrows clean.

3 How on earth does a worm accidentally bury a stone?
a) The stone rolls into a hole dug by the worm to catch beetles.
b) Worms push earth up from their burrows until the stone is covered.
c) Worms tunnel under the stone. The stone falls into the tunnel.

OUCH!

4 How long was the longest earthworm ever found?
a) 20 cm.
b) 45.5 cm.
c) 6.7 m.

5 Worms have a part of their body called a saddle. What on earth is it used for?
a) To give rides to earwigs.
b) To carry lumps of food.
c) To carry eggs about.

6 What happens when you cut a short piece off the end of a worm? (No need to try this out to discover the answer.)
a) It gets upset.
b) It grows a new tail.
c) It joins back together again.

7 What on earth do moles do to worms?
a) Eat them.
b) Bite their heads off.
c) Bite their heads off and let them escape.

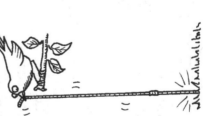

SCRUMMY!

Bet you never knew
You can 'charm' an earthworm. Every summer a primary school in Nantwich, England, hosts a weird competition. It's the world worm-charming championship. Yes – it's true. What a charming traditional pastime!

TWO THOUSAND AND THREE

NAME _____ DATE _____

Busy bees

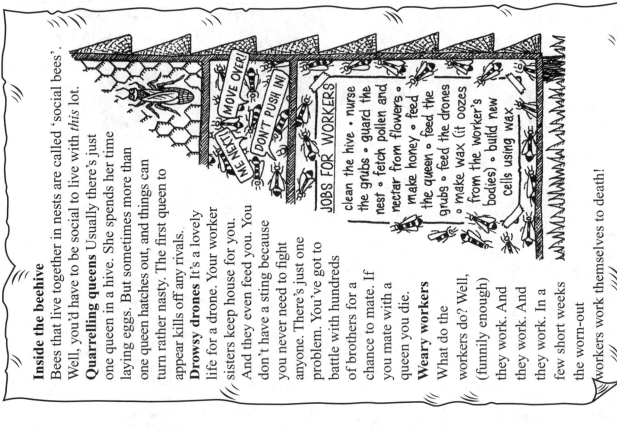

Inside the beehive

Bees that live together in nests are called 'social bees'. Well, you'd have to be social to live with *this* lot.

Quarrelling queens Usually there's just one queen in a hive. She spends her time laying eggs. But sometimes more than one queen hatches out, and things can turn rather nasty. The first queen to appear kills off any rivals.

Drowsy drones It's a lovely life for a drone. Your worker sisters keep house for you. And they even feed you. You don't have a sting because you never need to fight anyone. There's just one problem. You've got to battle with hundreds of brothers for a chance to mate. If you mate with a queen you die.

Weary workers What do the workers do? Well, (funnily enough) they work. And they work. And they work. In a few short weeks the worn-out workers work themselves to death!

JOBS FOR WORKERS

clean the hive • nurse the grubs • guard the nest • fetch pollen and nectar from flowers • make honey • feed the queen • feed the grubs • feed the drones • make wax (it oozes from the worker's bodies) • build new cells using wax

ME NEXT! MOVE OVER! DON'T PUSH IN!

Name of creature:	Bees and wasps
Where found:	Worldwide. Most bees live on their own. Only a few species live in large nests.
Horrible habits:	They sting people.
Any helpful habits:	Bees make honey and pollinate flowers.
Distinguishing features:	Thin waist between thorax and abdomen. Four transparent wings. Bees have long tongues and often carry yellow lumps of pollen on their hind legs.

BEE
TONGUE
NASTY STINGY BIT
WAIST
POLLEN

- Bees live in well-ordered communities where they have different jobs and strict rules!
- Use this sheet to help you recreate life in the hive.
- You could make a model or create an action drama.
- Ask your teacher for tips.

NAME _____   DATE _____

HORRIBLE HONEY

Horrible honey

So you love honey. Doesn't the thought of a lovely honey sandwich make your mouth water? And NOTHING is going to put you off it – right? RIGHT. Here's how bees make honey – complete with the horrible details.

1 Bees make honey from the sweet nectar produced by flowers. It's horribly hard work. Some bees collect from 10,000 flowers a day. They often visit up to 64 million flowers to make just 1 kg of honey.

2 That's good news for the flowers because the busy bees also pick up pollen. They even have little leg baskets to carry it. The bee takes the pollen to another flower of the same type. There, some of the precious pollen brushes on to the flower, fertilises it and so helps it form a seed.

POLLEN BASKETS

3 Why do you think the flower goes to all the bother of making scents, bright colours and nectar? Is it all for us? No! It's to attract bees. Lots of bees means lots of flowers. See?

4 A bee uses her long tongue and a pump in her head to suck up nectar. She stores the nectar in a special stomach.

LONG SLIMY TONGUE

5 Nectar is mostly water. To get rid of the water, bees sick up the nectar and dry it out on their tongues – ugh.

6 Then they store the honey in honeycomb cells until they need it. That's unless humans steal it for their sandwiches!

- Take a little honey out of the jar with a spoon and dab it on your observation plate. Feel and smell it. BUT DON'T EAT IT!

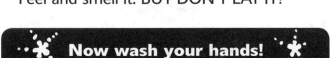
Now wash your hands!

- Describe what it looks, smells and feels like:

_____

_____

- What shape do you see repeated?

_____

- Why do you think that this is a better choice than a circle or pentagon?

_____

- Take a close look at the honeycomb. Draw what you see.

[blank box for drawing]

- Make a potato stamp of this shape to recreate the honeycomb pattern.

NAME _____   DATE _____

Terrible table manners!

Would you like to go to dinner with an insect? If so, you'd better learn how to eat like one.

What you need
A new sponge
Tape
A drinking straw
A saucer of drinking water

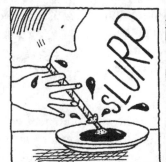 

What to do
1 Cut a small piece from the sponge.
2 Tape it to the end of the drinking straw.
3 Try to suck up a saucer of drinking water.
Congratulations! You're eating like a fly. Flies also sick up digestive juice. It helps them to dissolve their food before they slurp it up! (Don't try this!)

● Follow the instructions above and describe what happened.

● It felt like _____

_____

_____

● List the differences and similarities between the ways that insects, humans and animals eat.

Insects	Humans	Animals

NAME _____   DATE _____

DISGUSTING DESIGNS 1

Insect bits and pieces
Despite their many differences, insects have the same basic features.

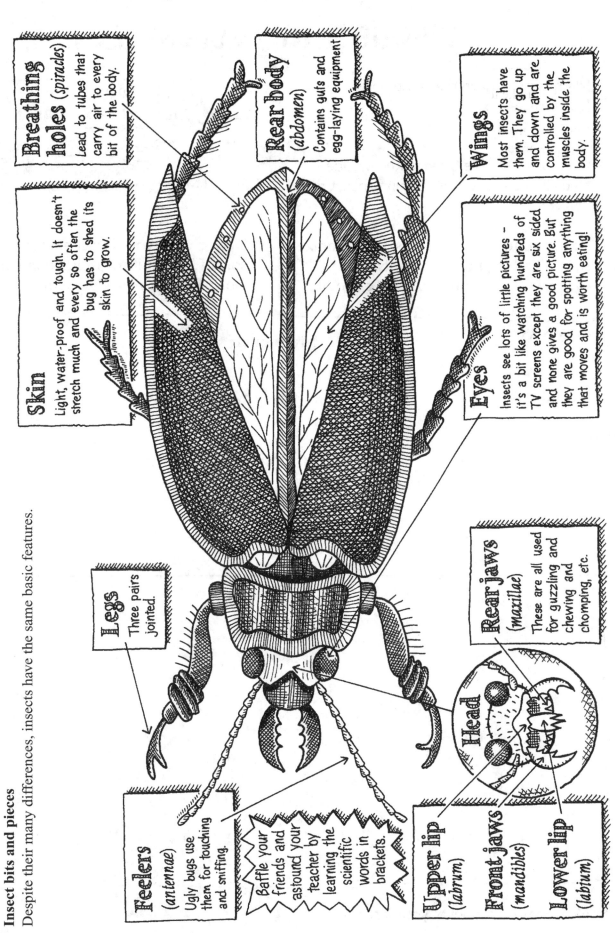

Breathing holes (*spiracles*)
Lead to tubes that carry air to every bit of the body.

Rear body (*abdomen*)
Contains guts and egg-laying equipment

Wings
Most insects have them. They go up and down and are controlled by the muscles inside the body.

Skin
Light, water-proof and tough. It doesn't stretch much and every so often the bug has to shed its skin to grow.

Eyes
Insects see lots of little pictures – it's a bit like watching hundreds of TV screens except they are six sided and none gives a good picture. But they are good for spotting anything that moves and is worth eating!

Legs
Three pairs jointed.

Rear jaws (*maxillae*)
These are all used for guzzling and chewing and chomping, etc.

Head

Feelers (*antennae*)
Ugly bugs use them for touching and sniffing.

Baffle your friends and astound your teacher by learning the scientific words in brackets.

Upper lip (*labrum*)

Front jaws (*mandibles*)

Lower lip (*labium*)

NAME _____ DATE _____

DISGUSTING DESIGNS 2

- Many insects have the same basic features... even if they don't like to admit it!

- Use your Horrible Science knowledge to design a completely original insect of your own.

- You need to include: feelers, legs, thorax, skin, breathing holes, abdomen, wings, eyes, rear jaws, front jaws, and a mouth.

I'D HATE TO BE A SNAIL – THEY'RE SO SLOW AND SLIMY

- Decide what your insect eats and what sort of habitat it might be found in. Don't forget to give it a name!

My insect:

Name:

Description:

Reproduces:

Typical lifespan:

Eats:

Habitat:

Draw your insect here

- Now make a model of your insect!

NAME _____ DATE _____

Nasty nursery rhymes

- This nursery rhyme is learned all over the world but... it is totally untrue! This is because:

  1 Ladybirds don't have homes. A sheltered leaf is good enough for them. So it is unlikely they would be bothered if their home *was* on fire.

  2 Ladybirds can fly but no ladybird would ever fly towards a fire. (Only maniac moths do that.)

  3 Ladybirds don't give two hoots about their children. Once their eggs are laid, that's that!

- This rhyme needs updating. Research what ladybirds do and where they live. Write down your research below and use it for an up-to-date and accurate Nasty Nursery Rhyme that tells the truth!

My research

1. Ladybirds can eat up to 100 greenfly each day.

2.

3.

4.

5.

Now write your rhyme!

_____

_____

_____

_____

_____

- Try the same for Little Miss Muffet!

NAME _____   DATE _____

Manic metamorphosis: The movie

Too horrible to watch

Films are full of insects – especially scary films. There are giant ants and giant flies. And it's amazing how many space monsters look like insects.

In fact, film designers often study ugly bugs to get good ideas for a really ugly monster.

But who needs made-up insect monsters when some real-life insects are far more creepy?

1 LITTLE INSECTS HATCH FROM EGGS

2 THEY DON'T LOOK LIKE THEIR PARENTS. INSTEAD THEY ARE REVOLTINGLY WRIGGLING THINGS CALLED GRUBS OR LARVAE. THESE CREATURES MAY EAT COMPLETELY DIFFERENT FOOD FROM THEIR PARENTS AND LIVE IN PLACES THEIR PARENTS WOULDN'T BE SEEN DEAD IN.

3 THE YOUNG GRUBS GUZZLE THEIR FOOD AND GROW UP AS FAST AS POSSIBLE.

4 THEY GO INTO HIDING IN A LITTLE CASE OR COCOON AND THEY COME OUT AS ADULT UGLY BUGS.

The scientific name for this hideous habit is 'complete metamorphosis'. Beetles, ants, bees and wasps, butterflies and moths, flies and mosquitoes go through a complete metamorphosis.

- Many minibeasts go through a scary transformation, even butterflies!

- Now you can turn this incredible plot into a blockbuster movie!

- Use paper and pens to make a flick book telling the story of a manic metamorphosis.

- Using the blank box, design a cover that will scare your friends and shock your enemies...

HORRIBLE SCIENCE

NAME _____   DATE _____

Ugly bug parade 1

- Take a look at these bugs. Look for the most revolting, disgusting, rancid creature that you can find ... and become it!

Earwigs 1,000 species. Earwigs get their name from the barmy belief that they crawl into your ears when you're asleep! They have mean-looking pincers at the back of their bodies. Males have curved pincers and females have straight ones.

Grasshoppers, crickets and locusts 20,000 species. They jump around and produce noises by rubbing their legs together to make themselves irresistible to the opposite sex.

Stick insects and leaf insects 2,000 species. Most live in tropical forests. Stick insects are so called because, well, they look like sticks, and leaf insects are so called because, you guessed it, they look like leaves. Either way they sit about all day looking like part of the furniture. Know anyone like that? It's a clever disguise, of course, but what a life!

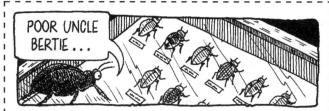

Beetles At least 350,000 species in this order worldwide – that's more than any other type of animal. But you'd never be able to catch them all in a jam jar. Apart from their vast numbers, many of them are known only as a single example in a museum collection.

Termites 2,000 species. Termites like a nice hot climate. They are small, soft insects but that doesn't mean they're a soft touch. Termites build nests that look like palaces and are ruled by kings and queens. Guard-termites are so serious about their work they sometimes explode in a bid to defend the nest!

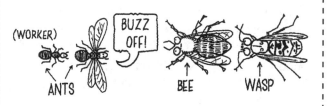

Ants, bees and wasps 100,000 species in this order worldwide. All members have a narrow waist between the thorax and the abdomen. Most have wings. (Worker ants don't develop wings – they're far too busy to go anywhere.)

NAME _____ DATE _____

Ugly bug parade 2

● Now take a look at *these* bugs. Which do you like best? Explain why.

_____

_____

Mantids and cockroaches 5,000 species. There's a strong family resemblance in their horrible habits. Cockroaches make midnight raids on the pantry. The praying mantis sits around cunningly disguised as part of a plant, and waits to pounce on its innocent victims.

Bugs 55,000 species in this order worldwide. They suck vegetable juices through straw-like mouths. Nothing ugly about that, you might think, except some do like a bit of blood now and then.

Flies 70,000 species in this order. They use one pair of wings for flying (which is what they do best). They also have the remnants of a second pair of wings, which look like tiny drumsticks and are actually used for balancing. Most Irritating Fly Habit: flying backwards, sideways and forwards round your head. OK – so you know they're incredible fliers already. Nastiest Fly Habit: some types of fly like nothing better than to lick the top of a big smelly cowpat. And then pay a visit to whatever you were going to have for tea.

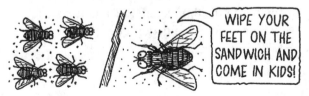

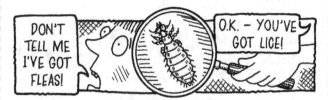

Sucking lice 250 species. Lice don't build their own homes. No. They live on other creatures. It's nice and warm there and you can suck a refreshing drop of blood whenever you feel like it. Lice live on all mammals except bats. Or at least no-one has ever found a louse on a bat.

Dragonflies, caddis-flies, mayflies are three different orders totalling 9,000 species. They start off living in water and then take to the air. Traditional names for dragonflies include 'horse stingers' and 'devil's darning needles'. Which is odd because they don't sting horses and you can't mend your socks with them.

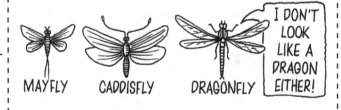

Butterflies and moths 165,000 species in this order worldwide. They have two pairs of wings and their young start off as caterpillars. Then they hide in a case called a chrysalis and re-arrange their body parts before emerging as butterflies or moths. It's a bit like you spending a few weeks taking your body apart in a sleeping bag. And then putting it all back together in a different order.

NAME _____ DATE _____

Ugly Bug Debate

My main points FOR / AGAINST banning bugs

My speech or questions

Our class vote

For:

Against:

- The motion is 'Should bugs be BANNED?'

- What do you think? It could be vital for votes!

Ugly bugs v. horrible humans: the debate
For every argument there are two points of view. And this is certainly true for ugly bugs and humans. See for yourself. Who do you sympathise with most – ugly bugs or humans?

Human point of view	Ugly bug point of view
Ugly bugs sting and bite us.	Humans trap us, poison us and experiment on us.
Ugly bugs eat our crops.	Humans destroy our food plants and plant their crops too close together so we've got nothing else to eat.
Ugly bugs creep into our homes.	Humans destroy our homes.
Ugly bugs spread diseases.	Humans spread pollution and rubbish.
Ugly bugs destroy our furniture.	To us it's only wood.
Ugly bugs cost us money.	Who cares about money?
They destroy our property.	Who cares about property?

NAME _____   DATE _____

Ugly Bug Debate: The campaign trail!

- Trying to win the vote for the bugs? This terrible but tasty menu may be just the thing to persuade undecided voters that the bugs are best!

Starters

Fried and salted termites
An African treat. Tastes like fried pork rind, peanuts and potato chips all mixed up!

L'escargots
Oui, mes amis! The traditional French delicacy. (Snails to you.) Fed on lettuce. Boiled and cooked with garlic, butter, shallots, salt, pepper and lemon juice. Served with parsley. Bon appetit!

Fried witchetty grub
A native Australian delicacy – these are giant wood-moth grubs. They look a bit like fusilli pasta and swell up when fried. Delicious!

Main courses

Stir-fried silkworm pupae
This tasty traditional Chinese dish is prepared with garlic, ginger, pepper and soy sauce. Wonderful warm nutty custard flavour. You spit out the shells. Very good for high blood pressure.

Roast longhorn timber beetle
Deliciously crunchy balsawood flavour. As cooked by the native people of South America.

Fried Moroccan grasshopper
Boiled bug bodies prepared with pepper, salt and chopped parsley then fried in batter with a little vinegar. You can also eat them raw.

Blue-legged tarantula
A popular spider dish in Laos in South-east Asia. Freshly toasted and served with salt or chillies. Flavour similar to the marrow in chicken bones.

Sweets

Mexican honeypot ants
A sweet sticky treat.

Baked bee and wasp grubs
An old recipe from Somerset in England. Juicy grubs baked in hot sticky honeycomb.

After your meal
Try one of our tarantula-fang toothpicks as used by the Piaroa people of Venezuela.

- Against those nasty bugs? Here's some filthy fly information that might just give your campaign wings!

- Now use all the dirty tricks you can to win this vital debate! Design a badge and poster to help persuade the electorate to vote your way.

Filthy Flies
They never give up. It doesn't matter how many times you let them out the window, they always come back.

1 Blowflies enjoy eating rotting meat and animal droppings. They lay eggs on rotting meat and even do terrible things to your Sunday roast.

ROAST CHICKEN – ALMOST AS TASTY AS CHICKEN DROPPINGS!

2 The common housefly has common table manners. It drops in for dinner uninvited and sicks up over its food. And then it's been known to serve up a free selection of over 30 deadly diseases.

NAME _____   DATE _____

MYSTERIOUS MALARIA

In the nineteenth century Scottish-born scientist Patrick Manson discovered how mosquitoes pass on malaria. Here's how he did it.

- Use this cartoon strip as the basis for a play. Include dialogue, stage directions, different scenes, music and costumes. Cast some actors as the mosquitoes and give them the opportunity to give their side of the story too! The first scene has been started for you:

Scene 1: Indian Medical Service office in London. Mrs Brady, Ronald Ross's secretary, is reading a newspaper with the headline 'Malaria still killing millions in India' as Patrick Manson enters.

Mrs Brady: (looking at him suspiciously) Yes? What do you want?
Patrick: I'm here to see Mr Ronald Ross if you please.
Mrs Brady: Ronald Ross? But he's a very important man you know, I doubt if he'll have the time–
Patrick: But I know him! Look! (holds up the headline) It's very important that I see him, I think I've got an idea, well I'm almost sure... that I've solved the mystery of malaria once and for all!

Mrs Brady: Solved the malaria mystery?! Don't make me laugh! If you had any idea of the number of people that claim that one each day... and all they want is the chance for a free trip to India on 'research' or whatever they call it. Blooming liberty! Never hear of them again usually...
Patrick: Maybe they die of malaria?
Mrs Brady: Less of your cheek if you don't mind, now, Ronald Ross is a very busy chap–
Ronald: (from behind Mrs Brady) –But never too busy to see an old friend like Patrick Manson!
Patrick: Ronald!
Ronald: Patrick! Great to see you, now please come into my office and tell me all about your new ideas. Oh and perhaps Mrs Brady could be so kind as to bring us a cup of her delicious tea!
Mrs Brady: (not very pleased) Certainly Mr Ross, it would be a ... pleasure.

- Now carry on the play with Scene 2 set in Ronald Ross's office...

NAME _____   DATE _____

BUG SAFETY

- Some animals and small creatures are poisonous to eat or can give us a rash if we touch them.

- Stone Age humans probably made some fatal mistakes!

- Design a poster for younger children explaining how they can live safely alongside minibeasts and show respect to our mutual habitats.

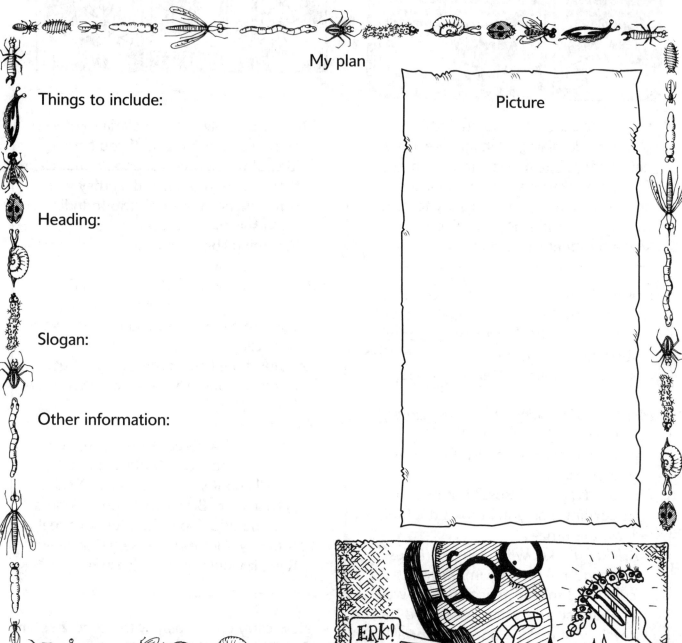

My plan

Things to include:

Heading:

Slogan:

Other information:

Picture

NAME _____   DATE _____

Maria Merien's world of brilliant bugs

- Maria Merien (1647–1717) was a Dutch scientist who was interested in drawing bugs. As there were no cameras at this time, drawings were particularly useful – and the only way that most people got to see plants and animals in far off countries.

Maria and her daughter Dorothy decided to go to Surinam and study bugs in the wild. This was an incredibly brave decision since it meant a hazardous voyage lasting several months with every danger of storms and pirate attack. And Surinam was known to be full of tropical diseases.

- Sometimes Maria wrote to her ex-husband back home. Here's what one of her letters might have looked like...

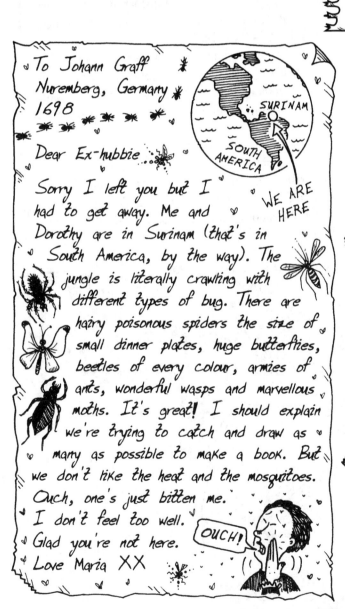

To Johann Graff
Nuremberg, Germany
1698

Dear Ex-hubbie

Sorry I left you but I had to get away. Me and Dorothy are in Surinam (that's in South America, by the way). The jungle is literally crawling with different types of bug. There are hairy poisonous spiders the size of small dinner plates, huge butterflies, beetles of every colour, armies of ants, wonderful wasps and marvellous moths. It's great! I should explain we're trying to catch and draw as many as possible to make a book. But we don't like the heat and the mosquitoes. Ouch, one's just bitten me. I don't feel too well. Glad you're not here.
Love Maria XX

SURINAM
SOUTH AMERICA
WE ARE HERE

OUCH!

- Look up South America in an atlas or on the internet.

- Contrast the minibeasts found there with those found in your country and write a letter to Maria telling her about the bugs near you.

Bet you never knew!
The native guides Maria hired liked a joke. They used to stick two halves of different bugs together and claim they had found a new kind of insect. Maria innocently drew these revolting remains for her book.

GOSH! A GIANT SNAIL-BEE. THANK YOU!

- You can also make up some bugs of your own to fool Maria!

NAME _____   DATE _____

Lethal lepidopterists

- Are you a lepidopterist? (lep-id-op-ter-ist = butterfly scientist)

1 How can you always tell a moth from a butterfly?
a) Moths come out at night and butterflies in the day.
b) Moths rest with their wings flat. Butterflies rest with their wings upright.
c) Moths don't have knobs on their antennae.

2 How does a hairstreak butterfly avoid having its head bitten off?
a) It has a dummy head.
b) It has a head with armour on it.
c) It bites first.

3 Silk comes from the cocoons spun by the silkworm moth caterpillar. According to legend this was discovered by a Chinese Empress in 2640 BC. But how did she make her discovery?

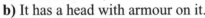

a) By careful scientific observation.
b) Her cat brought in a cocoon to show her.
c) A cocoon fell into her cup of tea.

4 Where does a cigar-case bearer caterpillar live?
a) In a cigar case.
b) In a little house made of bits of plants joined with silk.
c) In the fur of animals.

5 How can you tell when a butterfly is old?
a) Ragged wings
b) It goes grey.
c) Droopy feelers

I LOOK MORE LIKE A CABBAGE GREY!

Nowadays lepidopterists are mild-mannered folk who enjoy observing and photographing butterflies in what is left of their natural surroundings. It wasn't always like that.
1 In the eighteenth century, fashionable ladies wore brightly coloured butterfly and moth wings as jewellery.
2 Traditional butterfly hunters raced after butterflies with big nets shouting, 'There she goes!' When they caught an unfortunate flutterer they plunged it into a bottle of poison and pinned it to a board – horrible!
3 In the nineteenth century, hunters collected hundreds of butterflies from tropical forests in New Guinea. When the butterflies soared too high they fired guns loaded with fine shot to bring them down!
4 The British collector, James Joicey, spent a fortune over 30 years paying people to collect butterflies for him. By 1927 this millionaire's son had run out of cash. But when Joicey died in 1932 his collection numbered 1,500,000 dead butterflies.

AND TO MY FAMILY I LEAVE 1,500,000...

...DEAD BUTTERFLIES!

NAME _____ DATE _____

PLAGUE PUZZLE 1

1346 It came from the East and in the next six years 25 million people died. Peasants died in their fields and in England three Archbishops of Canterbury died in a single year. People lived in terror of THE BLACK DEATH.

1855 The plague ravaged China. In 1894 it hit the Chinese ports and in Hong Kong the death toll soared. The harbour was crammed with steam ships. And these ships took the disease to Japan, Australia, South Africa and the Americas. The plague reached India and killed six million people in ten years.

1898 In Bombay, Dr Paul-Louis Simond of the Institut Pasteur was a worried man. The fearless French doctor had been sent to India to find the cause of the plague. Day and night he wrestled with the same fiendish puzzle. In the stricken city thousands of people were dying. All developed fist-sized bulges under their armpits followed by fever and death. But how and why?

Day after day Simond scoured the squalid streets in search of an answer. Everywhere he noticed dead rats – 75 in one house. It was extremely unusual to find so many dead rats all together in one place.

They must have died quite quickly but what had killed them? And why was it that any humans who touched the rats seemed to fall sick with the plague? These plague rats seemed to have more fleas than healthy rats. And the fleas bit people, too.

The monsoon rain buffeted the outside of the makeshift lab in a tent. Inside Simond risked his own health as he cut up the dead rats. Then he made a dramatic discovery. In the rat's blood he found the germs known to cause the plague.

But what was the cruel connection between rats, fleas and humans? At long last the answer came. The intrepid scientist had solved the most terrifying mystery of all time. That evening he wrote in his diary in a frenzy of excitement.

But what was that crucial connection?
a) A flea bites a rat and gives it plague. The rat bites a human and passes on the plague.
b) A flea gets plague from biting an infected rat. The flea bites a human and passes on the plague.
c) A human gets plague from an infected flea bite. The plague-crazed human bites a rat and passes on the plague.

● What do you think? _____

_____

_____

NAME _____ DATE _____

PLAGUE PUZZLE 2

● My horrible hypothesis

NAME _____   DATE _____

INCREDIBLE BUG DISCOVERIES QUIZ

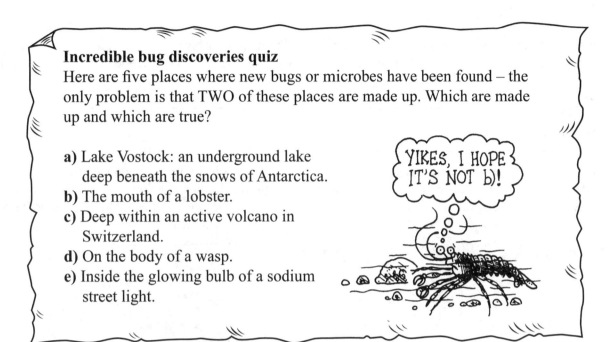

Incredible bug discoveries quiz
Here are five places where new bugs or microbes have been found – the only problem is that TWO of these places are made up. Which are made up and which are true?

a) Lake Vostock: an underground lake deep beneath the snows of Antarctica.
b) The mouth of a lobster.
c) Deep within an active volcano in Switzerland.
d) On the body of a wasp.
e) Inside the glowing bulb of a sodium street light.

YIKES, I HOPE IT'S NOT b)!

● How did you do? Now use your Horrible Science knowledge to add your own incredible bug and irritating insect questions for your partner to puzzle over.

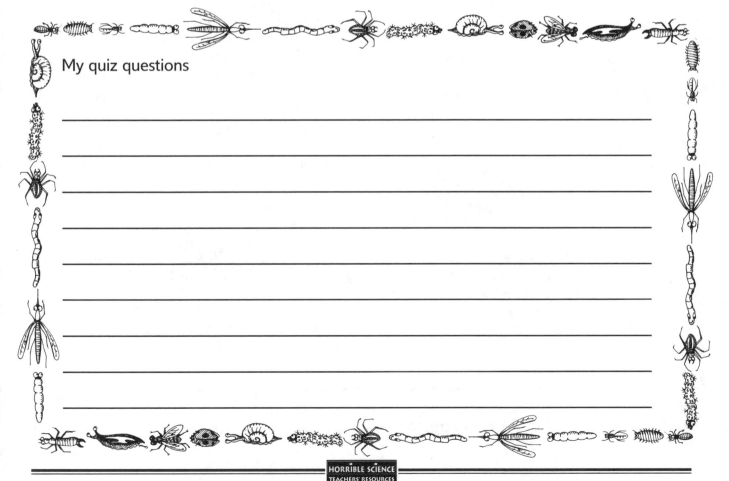

My quiz questions

_____

_____

_____

_____

_____

_____

_____

_____

_____

NAME _____   DATE _____

Unbelievable beetles!

With so many species of beetle it's inevitable that some of them are horribly amazing. And some of them have unbelievably horrible effects on human homes and food. But which of these beetles are too unbelievable to be true?

True or false?

1 The biscuit beetle eats, would you believe, biscuits. That's the bad news. The good news is that it doesn't like chocolate biscuits – only those nasty digestives you don't eat anyway.

2 The cigarette beetle eats (howls of amazement) cigarettes. Its larvae especially like the tobacco and they never take any notice of the health warnings.

3 The violin beetle *doesn't* eat violins – it just looks like a violin with legs. It lives amongst layers of fungus in trees in Indonesia.

4 The ice-cream beetle used to live in the Arctic where it ate small flies. More recently it has become a pest of cold stores where its favourite food is tutti-frutti ice cream.

5 'Tippling Tomm' is the nickname for a beetle that bores holes in wine and rum barrels. Tippling Tommy is actually a teetotaller. That's to say it never touches the alcohol inside the barrels – it prefers the wood!

6 The drug store beetle is the name given to a biscuit beetle that lives in medicine cabinets. It enjoys slurping up some medicines, including many poisons!

7 The giant gargling beetle is a rainforest beetle that takes a mouthful of dew and makes a loud gargling sound first thing in the morning.

8 The bacon beetle beats you to breakfast every time by looting your larder in the night and munching your meats. Its favourite food is – you guessed it . . . bacon!

9 The museum beetle is so fond of living in the past that it lives in dusty old display cases and eats museum specimens. Its favourite food . . . preserved ugly bugs.

10 Deathwatch beetles live in wood. Some English churches contain families of beetles that have lived there for hundreds of years.

● Now try out some of your own true or false questions on your partner.

NAME _____   DATE _____

Insect news quiz

Welcome to the first newspaper exclusively for insects. Can you spot the FOUR silly factual mistakes?

NAME _____   DATE _____

fold here

Answers (total score eight points):

1 TRUE. The course is just 30 cm long.

2 FALSE

3 TRUE. They're particularly good at tasting sugar and in fact the fly's feet are many times better at tasting than your tongue.

4 TRUE. The female fly can sense grubs cowering beneath the bark. It drills its egg-laying tube through the wood and spears the grubs before laying its eggs inside their living bodies. The eggs hatch into ichneumon grubs and eat their hosts alive!

5 FALSE. The mysterious chocolate disappearances in your house may have something to do with your mum.

6 TRUE. The mouse-eating spider of South America rubs its legs hard to make a cloud of tiny hairs that stick in the flesh and cause a burning pain.

7 TRUE. The attacker eats the guts and the sea cucumber escapes to grow more guts. Yes – this fact is really hard to stomach!

8 TRUE. Believe it or not, she taught her spiders to spell the word 'HI' in their webs and she has also taught a swarm of bees to land on top of her head in the shape of a hat. Maybe she's just got a bee in her bonnet...

● Now use your Horrible Science knowledge to research your own Ugly Bug Quiz questions.

Bet you never knew
People used to believe that insects such as flies developed from rotting meat and dead animal bodies. What a nice thought!

UGLY BUG QUIZ

This is a straightforward quiz – you just say TRUE or FALSE to each question. But there's an ugly twist: for each wrong answer you LOSE a point. For this reason you need someone to read you the quiz and keep note of your score!

1 A magathon is a maggot race organized by the World Organization of Racing Maggots (WORM) at Barney's Bar in Montana, USA. TRUE or FALSE?

> THAT'S ONLY HALF A MAGGOT – WHERE D'YOU FIND IT?

> IN THAT APPLE YOU ATE AT LUNCHTIME

2 Insects have been found living on Mars (that's the planet not the chocolate bars). TRUE or FALSE?

3 Blow flies can taste food through their feet. TRUE or FALSE?

4 Mind you, that's nothing – an ichneumon (ick-noy-mon) fly can *hear and smell* through its feet. TRUE or FALSE?

> YOU'LL HAVE TO SPEAK UP. I'VE GOT MY SHOES ON.

5 The chocolate beetle only eats chocolate. It sneaks into houses and can scoff a whole bar by itself. TRUE or FALSE?

6 Tarantula spiders fire tiny spears at mice. TRUE or FALSE?

7 The sea cucumber is a kind of sea slug that defends itself by squirting its guts over an attacker. TRUE or FALSE?

8 Felicity Whitman of Arizona, USA, has taught spiders to spell words in their webs and ants to nibble patterns in lettuce leaves. TRUE or FALSE?

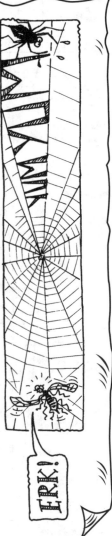

> ERK!